A FRESH SQUEEZE ON DATA

ON DATA

PROBLEM SOLVING WITH DATA

One sunny day, Clara runs home and tells her family:

BIG NEWS! I want to raise money for the hospital. I'm going to open a lemonade stand!

Can I help?

Sure, you're great at making signs!

The next day, Clara and Alex wake up early. They set up a table with a sign in front of their house. They lay out a jug of fresh lemonade and a stack of cups.

No one bought lemonade from them for two hours. Alex looks sadly at his sister and says,

Lemonade

#1.00

Clara begins to think about what she might have missed in her planning. What could she have done differently to bring more people to their lemonade stand?

Suddenly, Clara has an idea.

Clara thinks about how her mom solves problems at work. Her mom is a data scientist and works at a company that uses data to solve all kinds of problems.

Data can tell us what people want to buy at our lemonade stand. We don't have any data yet. We have to collect data by asking questions.

What questions?

Let's ask our friends what they would want to buy at a lemonade stand.

Clara and Alex ask their friends what they would buy at a lemonade stand.

Clara and Alex talk to their friends Carlos, Isabella, and Ethan. Carlos wants strawberry lemonade. Isabella wants stickers for her notebooks. Ethan wants regular lemonade and some painted rocks for his garden.

Clara and Alex go back home to collect stickers and paint rocks.

Hoping to get more visitors to their lemonade stand, they reopen with lemonade, stickers, and painted rocks.

They wait and wait but only sell two cups of regular lemonade.

Mr. Williams, their mom's coworker, sees them looking sad at their stand.

Why are you all so sad?

Hi, Mr. Williams. Our things are not selling well. We asked our friends what we should sell, but it didn't help.

Clara and Alex begin asking people they meet in the neighborhood, adults and kids.

The neighbors give Clara and Alex lots of different answers about what they'd like to buy, including cookies, cupcakes, lemonade, stickers, painted rocks, and yo-yos! No other people ask for strawberry lemonade.

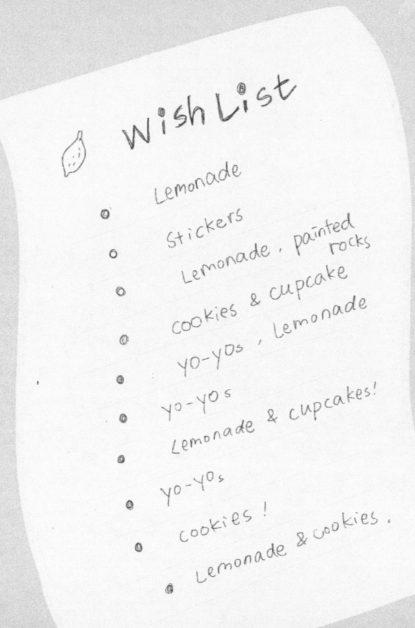

What three things do people want most?

Item	Number
Lemonade	5
stickers	1
painted rocks	1
cookies	3
cupcakes	2
yo-yos	3

Our neighbors want freshly squeezed lemonade, cookies, and yo-yo's the most. Let's sell these things at our lemonade stand!

Not many people walk past our house. Let's gather our friends and look for places that have more people walking by.

Clara and Alex meet up with Noah, Lucas, and Mia, who are all excited to join the Lemonade Crew!

Noah lives by the grocery store, Lucas lives across from the park, and Mia lives near the school.

Let's count how many people go by our houses in one hour.

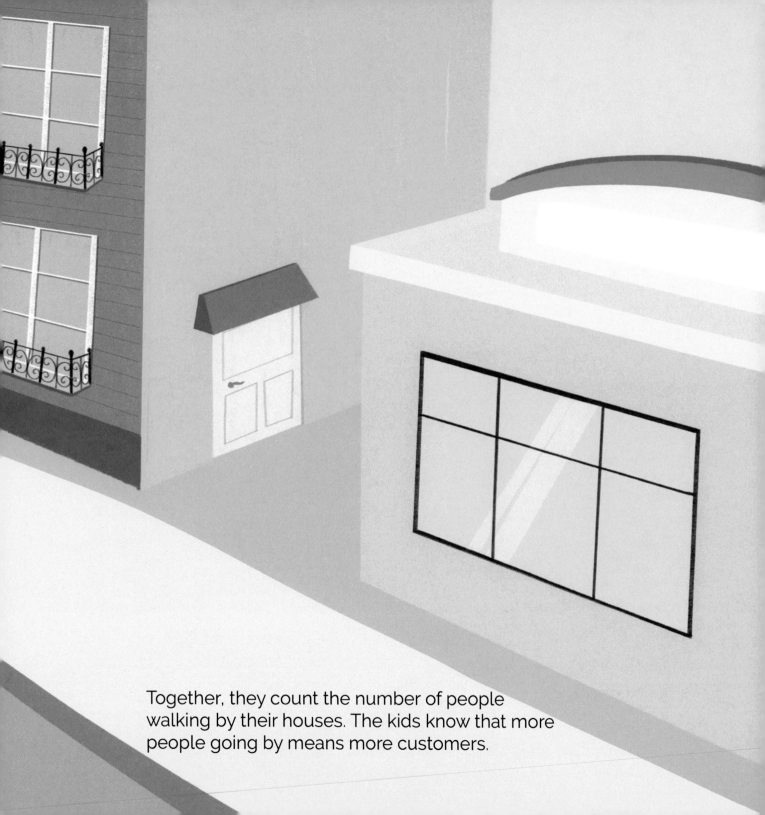

Together, they count the number of people walking by their houses. The kids know that more people going by means more customers.

LOCATION	☻
Noah's house (store)	35
Lucas' house (park)	56
Mia's house (school)	21

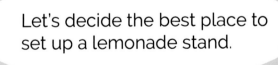

Let's decide the best place to set up a lemonade stand.

Can you link the correct place to the chart?

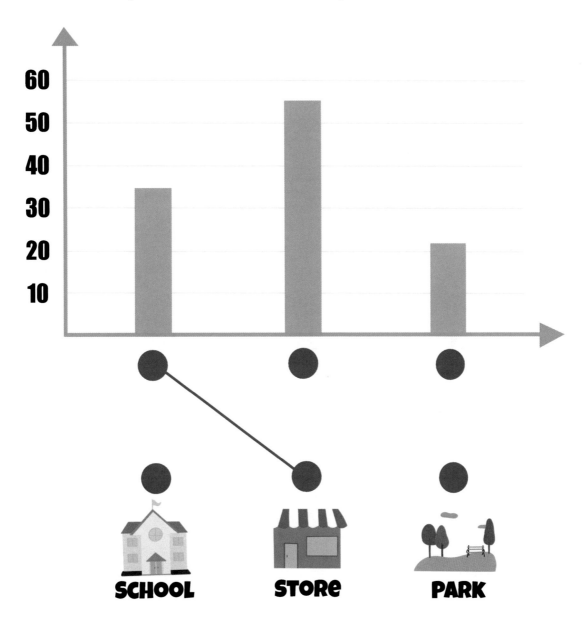

Which location had the most people passing by?

Clara and Alex realize that Lucas' house is the best place to set up the lemonade stand. It is right across the street from the park where the most people are walking by.

Today is the big day! Mia and Lucas work hard to squeeze the lemons. Noah and Clara bake the cookies. Alex carefully lays out all the yo-yo's.

The Lemonade Crew has so many customers,
and everyone is busy!

At the end of the day, the kids are excited about how much they have raised.

Clara and Alex's mom and dad come and help the kids clean.

We're so proud of you!

The next day, the kids give the hospital a big
envelope with a letter and all the money they raised.

Everyone is so proud of the good things they have done. The Lemonade Crew now understands the power of data science. They are on their journey to make the world better using data!

Please use this money to help people get better.

♥ — the Lemonade Crew

CAN YOU TELL US MORE ABOUT DATA?

 Data scientists teach **self-driving cars** to recognize things on the road.

 Like people, cars, and traffic lights?

You're right! Lanes, turn signals, everything a human driver needs to know about.

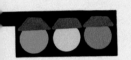

SELF-DRIVING

But how do you teach a car?

We help train the computer in the car to make decisions. We give it **labels**, so it can put things into different groups, or what data scientists call **classes**.

I can label these images!

Great job! A computer has to see a ton of images with labels like these to learn new things.

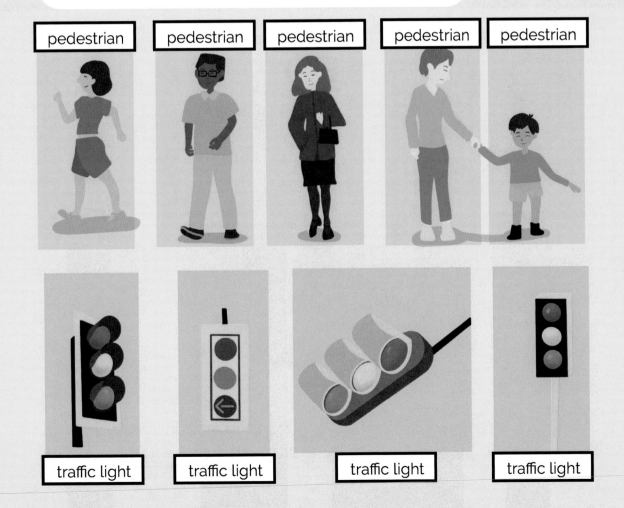

Can computers learn without labeled data?

Yes! We can also teach a computer to learn from patterns. You and I can look at lemons and strawberries and know they're different kinds of fruit without anyone telling us.

INPUT

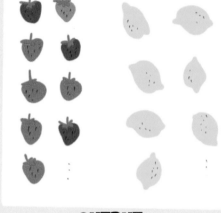

OUTPUT

We give computers enough information or **input** to provide the answers, or **output**, we want.

When we use patterns, we won't have the data labeled for the computers, but we have millions of images that can provide features for computers to look at.

If we give the computer a lot of images of lemons and strawberries and ask the computer to separate these images into two categories, the computer could look at the color, shape, or other features that the images provide.

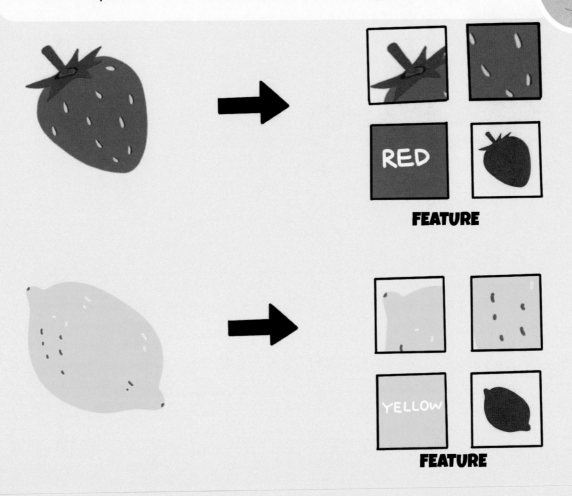

FEATURE

FEATURE

But where do we get all the data that we want?

We ask people questions and watch what they do. It's just like what you did with the lemonade stand, Clara and Alex. You asked what people wanted to buy and then saw what they actually bought.

We also learned that we need to ask both kids and adults for information for our lemonade stand.

If you only include one group of people's ideas, the data that you collect could be biased. **Bias** means that the data doesn't give a fair picture of what all the people think. We need to hear more people's voices because the decisions we will make might affect them as well.

How might kids' taste in food be biased?

How does this data help us in our daily lives?

There are so many ways that data helps every aspect of our lives. Part of the data scientist's job is to collect the desired data to solve problems.

I love music. Can data help me with music?

Yes. With data collected from your playlist, we can help computers recommend the next song that you might like.

I want to be a doctor when I grow up. Can data help me with medicine?

Yes. With the data collected from patients, researchers can study and find cures for new diseases. Besides music and medicine, data science helps people make better decisions.

For example, we **predict** the amount of milk people might buy next week at the grocery store, so the store knows how much to stock. We predict the traffic in the next hour and find the fastest way to get you to your school in the morning.

ReAL-WORLD PROBLeMS

Data scientists use data and similar methods to solve larger problems that affect more people.

Try the activities below. Use data to answer the questions.

Question:
Which type of video game should a company create?

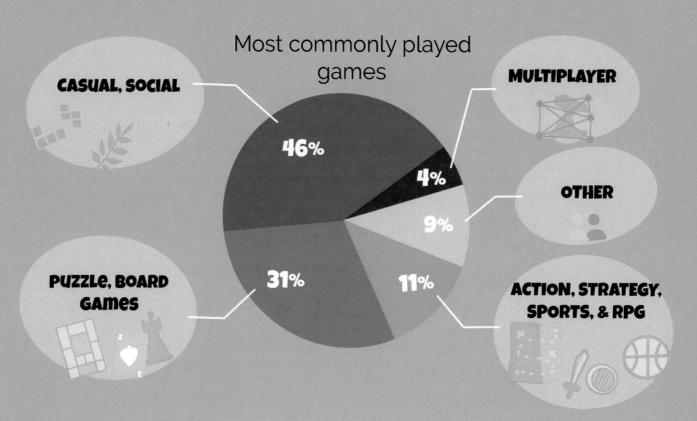

Most commonly played games

CASUAL, SOCIAL

MULTIPLAYER

OTHER

PUZZLE, BOARD GAMES

ACTION, STRATEGY, SPORTS, & RPG

46%

4%

9%

31%

11%

Answer:

Question:
How does data help my deliveries arrive faster?

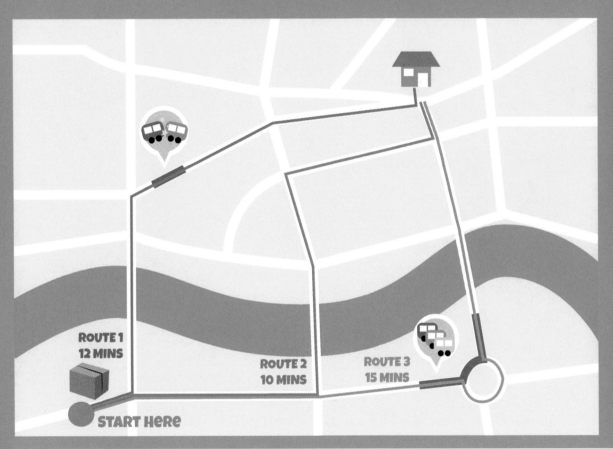

ROUTE 1
12 MINS

ROUTE 2
10 MINS

ROUTE 3
15 MINS

START HERE

Answer:

Question:
How can I use data to identify a dog's breed?

Hint: What are some of the features of each breed?

Answer:

Question:
Can data science help cure diseases?

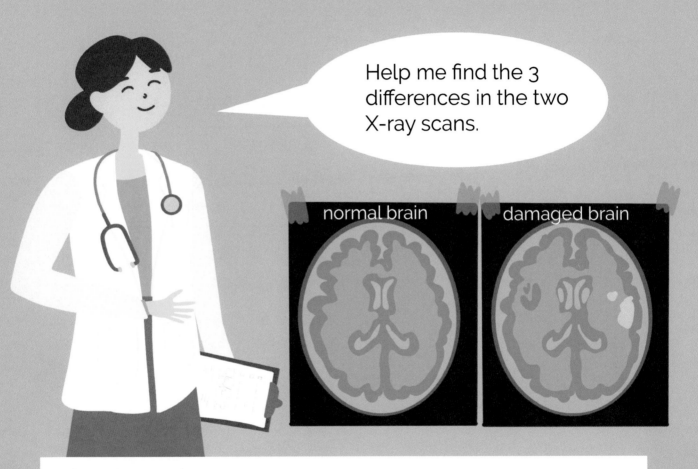

Answer:

Question:
How do we decide what food to take to space?

	mass (how much space does the food take up)	calories (how much energy can it provide)
FOOD A	100	200
FOOD B	50	150
FOOD C	200	250

Answer:

Can you think of one question that you want to answer with data:

My question is:

A Letter to the Reader

Hello Everyone,

Thank you so much for reading this book! My sons, Flynn and Jedd, and I really enjoyed learning from Clara and Alex and hope you did too.

In our world, it's very important that we understand where data comes from and how it can be used to make good predictions and decisions. Data can help us find the best solutions for people, our natural resources, and our communities. There are a lot of problems we can solve by analyzing data. The possibilities are limitless – just as they are for you!

Thanks for starting early on your path to appreciating the value of data and developing your data literacy. You're on your way – keep it going!

Scott Aronson
Proud father of two young boys &
Chief Operating Officer at Cloudera

GLOSSARY

Bias (Data bias): The available data does not fairly represent the people or objects in the study.

Classes: The different groups that we sort things into.

Data: A collection of facts or things you know, such as numbers, words, images, or just descriptions of things.

Input: Information given to the computer. In computer science, inputs are usually data you wish to analyze.

Labeled data: Information that has been tagged with one or more labels, such as a picture of a cat with the label "cat".

Output: Data generated by a computer. In machine learning, outputs are predictions generated by the model. Usually, output changes when the input is changed.

Predict: To guess about what you think will happen.

Self-driving cars (autonomous car): A vehicle that is capable of sensing its environment and moving by itself.

Unlabeled data: Data that comes with no tag. For example, a picture of a cat without the label "cat".

www.freshsqueezekids.com

www.readyai.org/a-fresh-squeeze-on-data

Contributors: Annabel Hasty, Dave Tourezky, Ethan Chen, Joel Wilson, Juno Schaser, Kelli Lawless, Madge Miller, Melanie Beck, Roozbeh Aliabadi, Santiago Giraldo, Sushil Thomas

Author and Illustrator: Shanshan Jin

Made in the USA
Middletown, DE
27 October 2021